Matters of
Love and Death

OTHER BOOKS BY
ROBERT GITTINGS

LITERARY CRITICISM

John Keats
John Keats: The Living Year
The Mask of Keats
The Keats Inheritance
Shakespeare's Rival
The Living Shakespeare (editor)

PLAYS AND POEMS

The Makers of Violence
Out of this Wood
Wentworth Place
Famous Meeting
This Tower my Prison
Matters of Love and Death

MATTERS OF LOVE AND DEATH

by

ROBERT GITTINGS

HEINEMANN
LONDON

Heinemann Educational Books Ltd
LONDON EDINBURGH MELBOURNE TORONTO
SINGAPORE JOHANNESBURG AUCKLAND
IBADAN HONG KONG NAIROBI

SBN 435 14357 3

First published 1968
Reprinted 1969

Published by
Heinemann Educational Books Ltd
48 Charles Street, London W1X 8AH
Printed in Great Britain by
Morrison and Gibb Ltd
London and Edinburgh

Contents

Acknowledgements are due to the BBC, *The Listener*, *The Times Literary Supplement*, *The Critical Quarterly*, *The New Statesman*, *The Anglo-Welsh Review* and *Outposts*.

By the Lake

A Sequence based on
Frieda and D. H. Lawrence
at Lake Garda

I

Lying in bed I watch the sunrise
Pale as matchflame beyond the mountain,
Dim and milky the mist-filled lake;
Then at a keyhole spot on the ridge
The sky throbs gold; a burning-glass,
It blobs and fuses the rocky groove;
It sharpens, white-hot, a needle shimmer,
The probing lamp in a welder's hand,
The intense, the molten, the living light.
In a spangle and sizzle of spark, it hits
The transfixed water, the workman day
Laying the racing-track of the sun
Broad and smooth on the pitchblend surface,
A road to follow, wake and get up,
To be a man in the march of day,
Only myself and the dawning world,
As other men wake, unslotting the planks
From the lemon-gardens' roof, or perched
On the high stiff centipede of a ladder
Tending olives, all men to their work
And I to mine. In the dappled room
Behind me, a murmur; a cheek turns
This way, that, on the smashed-in pillow,
Tumble of hair. My vagrant eyes
Still gorged with sun, my shaken heart
Still dazed with change, can either see
If the tangled head is dark or fair?
I turn from the window. The world is here.

II

Remember now the night,
Now while she lies in bed,
Remember who it was who said
'Take me for ever':
Not her.

Remember now the love,
And every move and cry,
Remember one who seemed to die,
Scarcely recover;
Not her.

Remember now the pain
Of parting, and the hard
Memory, every feeling barred,
In which I locked the past
To last,

And came to this, a love
More like a battlefield,
Bed stripped, and stained with blood unhealed,
Yet at love's centre,
Alone, her.

III

The blonde aristocrat with a Rubens body
Lies in my working day-bed,
This high-bred aboriginal, whose loveways
Shatter my labouring morals
Just as I shocked to passionate requital
That dark neat-headed other,
Who lies so far from this Italian autumn,
Remote in time's changed season
That severs lovers wider than the sea.

If they could meet, how would they mix in common?
This, the imperial lady
Talking de haut en bas to humble people,
A sunflower condescension:
That, the wind-petal trembling over the slag-bank,
Root-clung to my raw clinker,
Part of my growing-up. Memories' collision
Explodes my mind each morning.
Body for body they have met in me.

IV

Till late in the morning was mist;
The fisherboats hung on the lake
With their still sails floating in air
Like magic or African birds,
Flamingo and ibis and crane
Flocked down to the water to drink.

The siesta steamer rocked by,
Then the surface twinkled and cleared;
In the four o'clock afternoon cool
We took our boat from the quay;
With the hiss and drip of the oars
I rowed you out from the land.

The snowy mountains looked up
Reversed in that glassy pool;
My blade-stroke rippled the summit.
You sat, beautiful, calm
As day and ripe as the season,
All weathers and times in one.

That moment, suspended in truth,
My heart turned over to see
The woman created in you,
Mistress and mother and wife,
Nothing competing or lost,
Given complete to my care.

Now on the headland we lie
At the twisted olive's root,
Sunset flooding the water
And the far peaks rosy-pink.
The vines are yellow and red,
The fig-trees spiked with flame,

Cyclamen drop their blood
In the clefts of the shadowy hills,
Fishermen, standing up,
Row inward with silver glint,
The new moon prises free
And lights pulse out, low down.

Love, love, stay ever like this,
Full and fierce and yet whole,
Love where a man can work,
And a woman be all herself:
I touch your arm, and we walk
Close-linked to our home below.

V

My love in England's a gypsy. I alone
Could not have taught her passion. Some must come
From the side-snatches of heredity:
That loose, land-owning horseman riding home
Liked the look of the girl who handed a drink,
Roughed her into the barn on the pricking hay,
And thrust his reckless seed into your strain –
Those times you fought me back, brazen and gay.
Then there's your classic head and pose: I see
Signs of it here in their straight backs, proud eye,
Some Roman coining centuries long ago
Regal in peasant scarf: or in a gallery,
One of those so-called virgins Raphael painted,
Really the girl from the bakery, so like you
It stops my throat and makes me blush like a boy
To meet in naked paint what I alone knew.

VI

Weather should warn us. The weird black cloud
Trailing low over the lake
Tried to, but we were stubborn; snake
On the water, it puffed and swam; about
The same moment the lightnings split out,
Your anger showed,

A flash at first. Still I was not warned,
Joked, mentioned names. A blow
Like furnace-breath stopped me, blasted: you,
I'd never seen you. Blank like the sheets
Of lightning, a staring stranger meets
My smile unreturned.

A hate like the steaming water, now
The serpent-headed rain
Hits, but hot, no cool touch; again,
Again, actual fists, beating my face,
Words torrenting down, no stopping-place,
Bruising cheek, brow,

A grey wall through which a madwoman
Speaks endless diseased logic,
Mad past with gobbets to make you sick
Of love's dead children devoured, phrases
That stick with perverted animal faces,
No aspect human.

A panic joy, as I know since,
Releases her to do this,
Torment our marriage-bed intimacies,
Tear them, expose them to violent test,
Exulting that only what is best
She can make wince.

So the suffering a woman must inflict
By being fixedly blind
To a man, when anger eats her mind,
Is mine now. I am fully paid
For all I carelessly did or said
In my neglect.

Moved, as pride and weakness can move
A self-concerning man,
I did not see what I began.
I see now. While total storm roars
Its insane cataract, outdoors, indoors,
This too I must love.

VII

Worm in my side, raw worm
That burrows red in flesh,
Reminder of my term
Of life, the ticking drip
Leaking my time away.

You are my secret, held
Captive between scarred ribs;
I am your host and shield
And your rebellious food,
Wizening where you grow.

Diurnally you send
Your spinning nauseas up
So that I retch and rend
The bright day turned to bile
Bittering lung and heart.

Yet through your tremors, I
Taste the truth's olive tang;
This way we train to die,
With all we see and do
Companioned by that fact.

Since you will not remove,
I accept life with you,
And since the death of love
Is preparation for death,
I shall then be prepared.

VIII

The shore-patrolling mountains wear
Their shoulder-capes of snow,
While Christmas roses mass and glow
In white reflecting air.

I heave in wood and heap the fire
Till the flames lift and flap,
Wild figures springing the furnace trap,
Marionettes without wire.

Outside our closed and coppery room
The winter shadows strip,
Inside, your body, breast and hip,
Sharp hairs and guarded womb,

Flesh, the illusion, origin
Of so much waste and shame,
The spark blown by another's name,
Ember that gnaws within,

The inferno of past love; and yet
Some coal from hell can shake
Its lamp, dot-dashing on our lake
Love's code of no regret.

IX

A winter interlude: the players reach
Our lakeside village, like
A peasant company of Shakespeare's day,
And even in Italy it must be his play –
Hamlet, no less.

In the stage-box, mysterious Englishman,
I sit as honoured guest,
Come from the villa of night sobbing, now
Dressed in dark suit with intellectual brow
Hamlet himself,

And look down at my drama's counterpart,
Gross-necked Italian lout,
Baggy and trailing disgusting greasy crepe,
Yet in the shuddering poetry's foreign rape
Hamlet is here.

'O that this too-too solid flesh – ' I drop
A programme, hide a grin,
And there she enters with her eyes of black,
Chalk face, dark hair that waterfalls her back,
Hamlet's desire.

' – would melt' – what then of her young breasts and
    womb?
I did not write this scene,
Yet I have acted it a thousand ways,
And so has he that now my hero plays,
Hamlet the man.

To make some woman suffer, then declare
'I love her' is our aim;
The Galahad of purity and trust,
The Lancelot of valour and of lust,
Hamlet is both.

'Go to a nunnery, go' – those words, exact,
I wrote, or said, or meant,
And never guessed the river flowed so deep,
Nor girls like willows could bend down and weep –
Hamlet aghast.

The skull, the graveyard, the envenomed blade,
I view the rest through tears;
Though the great soul angelically dies,
Haunted by that white face, those drowning eyes,
Hamlet sits, damned.

X

And should I write to her?
Yes, if I will, why not?
We endlessly discuss
The echo of that name,
So why not write it down?

Your name, by the hard frost of absence nipped,
An eight-years' heartache chiselled in the script.

And what next should I say?
A quondam lover, I
Am dumb for language, so
Essay a flippant note,
Not show the whole of heart.

It hasn't been all roses, love, I fear;
Then, I can't afford roses; they're too dear.

Yes, but the rest breaks through.
Though I set down mere fact,
The postscript of a cry
Rises between the lines,
What I should wish to be –

If you would come and live with us, if we
Somehow could share this core of love, all three.

Impossible in sense,
But to my logic true.
Stamp it, post it. The flap
Falls like a snap of jaw –
If I could take it back –

No taking back, once we have lived with it,
The folly and the harm love can commit.

XI

From the little ledge where the lake washes
We hoped to clamber the hanging cliffs,
Guided by paths to a perilous gallery,
Sheer rock over a shrunken ridge.
We like flies on a flattened wall,
I terrified, she triumphant,
Elate on heights with her level head,
I ever drawn to the downfalling edge.
Proud to put me in panic, she presses
On: I stagger, stumbling after,
Fearing loss, afraid to be alone,
Ashamed to show my manhood halting.
She, angry, abrupt, shouts back,
Furiously stubborn, steps faster,
Contest now increasing to conflict,
Not wishing death but willing destruction
To other's sexhood, hardy for self.
Weakening, I wonder: why not end it
Like Oates outgoing to save Scott,
Submit to her ego by easy suicide,
Accident amply apt to explain,
Quietus to the incurable quarrel
Between our souls, what better solution?
Or – fantasy fast becoming frantic –
Suppose she slip, her own forced fault,
Trying to torment me, find fatality?
Ghastly pastime, to play with the grim
Master of men and women: once moved

To strike, his ice-dart sticks indeed,
And we in wanton disaster dead,
Dead, dead. The rolling echoes reverberate.
Lifting foreheads, we find on an upland
Our feet tread flat with trembling faintness.
After ordeal, drama's achievement,
Sudden peace possesses our spirits,
Passed through horror to hope for plenty.
In a refuge of rocks, on a silver snowfield,
Tenderly close we cling together;
Breath of both reviving our love,
Mute we kiss where we might have killed.

XII

Like an unwanted child,
Caesarian then stillborn,
Dead illegitimacy,
My letter stares at me,
Cold eyes no one can mourn,
Stiff limbs awkwardly stilled.

So she returns the long
Revelation of love,
In one unworded post
Writes off our pentecost,
This envelope enough
To blanket every tongue.

Yet dumb negation is
With some a kind of act:
The near-trapped animal
Escapes if it can call
Darkness down on the fact
To cover where it lies.

She has evaded terror,
Leaving me quick with mine,
I with my dangerous hope,
Halter or mountain-rope,
Trust the hard-tested twine
To drag me clear of horror.

Love, strengthen now your links
To meet the double strain;
If one accept my cost,
And one, thinking me lost,
Can find her peace again,
Let it be as she thinks.

XIII

As we wake by the lake once more
A pink dawn presses the pane,
Not dayshine's sallow return,
The account to be answered again:
Close it; and open the door.

Flesh of the Spring, almond flower
Nude in the new blue sky,
The apricot-coloured air
Washes us through, you and I
One body, seraph of fire.

Then climb where the mule-track shows
Its tortoise-back wriggle of stone;
The gulleys are charged with green,
The rubble-locked streams rush down,
The heat is hunting the snows,

Winter in retreat; we have made
The first mile of love's advance,
Hardest but best. The roofs
Below with their freckled dance
Tomb our lost hours in their shade.

All light now, light between rocks
As higher we climb, flooded pools
Of sulphur, primrose in strength,
And the grave white violet that cools
The eye with serious looks,

Bright flowers full of stars and bells,
Myriad, devious, love's self
Pictured in natural disguise;
Even thrown on the rocky shelf
Love's tenuous seedhold dwells.

Even where the landslip's gash
Murders the hillside, a bird,
Nightingale, angel and hope,
Resounds till nothing is heard
But the cry that echoes our flesh.

Look now, we have come out above
Hate, out on the headland bluff.
We stare at the floor of the lake.
Could we have lived there? Enough
We two have come through to love.

We have come through now; equal
We live with the past put by.
We fought but did not destroy.
There is all time left to try.
Grief, grief: but love is the sequel.

Matters of Love and Death

Dame School

FOR JO

This is the road you came along, the road
You crossed, then the cut
Through the spinney, fields on both sides, until
The curved shrubbed wall of the big-house garden led
The last small lap to school,
The boxed-in building, no more than a good-sized hut.

Never mind size, nor that those old ladies, true,
Had no science to teach,
Nor theory at all, unless one can class and subsection
The heart, by whose individual lessons they drew,
Instinct their only selection,
Knowledge from every child through the child in each.

Stubborn square brows and fists that could fly outside,
Now clamped round pens,
Tongues between teeth, each day a flavour, each one
Maplike coloured by some disaster or pride,
At bedtime to savour or shun,
And the school an added limb, an extra sense,

Existing yet, though our adult world disguises
With reason and fact
The stories that those old voices told as truth:
Still like a dew-mist on the field-path rises
The past, transfixed in youth,
The letters that spelt your first name, your initial act.

You carry it with you still, like the classroom flowers,
Satchel or shoes
You carried then, sufficient care for a child
To learn the burdens that grow invisibly ours,
And the way through the new-mown field
Remains the only way you can never lose.

August 1914

My father had the telegram when I
Could barely read. An autumn victory,
The voices sang, embarked at midnight: then
Silence, massively emptied of its men.
Black ribs of newsprint bulked across the page.
Night fears kept me awake; it was my age,
But whispers too, and once an earthquake noise
Smelling of cordite after. Closed to boys
The foreshore, barbed with sentries. A cap came
Bobbing the waves; we dared; a German name
Rewarded trespass. So began the tide
Of questions no one answered. Summer died
Into a labyrinth without guiding rope,
Good times mislaid. Groping through adult hope,
I held my childhood on a four-year lease
Till in red chalk the pavements shouted Peace.

Halfway

At halfway house, the table set,
I and my latter self have met.
Through narrow eyes, not unconcerned,
I watch what will not be unlearned,
The habits hasty or slow-grown,
All his, though only half my own: –
The sapling temper that soon is
A rough-barked tree; the histories
Of small account that have become
Obsession's legend; all the sum
Whose digits score their way to tens
Of silent-pointing evidence.
How can I question? or how ask
This older frame that bears my mask
Where this crept in or that was dropped,
Why in that part the pulses stopped?
How else but force my sight away
From future doubt to present day,
How else but on heart's precipice
Look steady down the soul's abyss?

A Daughter

A daughter in my middle age
Tears a bar out from that cage
Where labour, habit, lassitude
Lock up a life for dubious good.
Small digit growth, you have become
An extra number in the sum,
The plus and minus of mankind
Where we our sole relation find;
For though of continents we speak
The heart in Asia does not break,
Nor on Formosan islands lose
That peace which our four walls enclose.
The huge map of a hundred creeds
That suffers, angers, triumphs, bleeds,
Touches at most our outward cells.
The main self, where distinction dwells,
Is shut apart, a room prepared
For those in whom one flesh is shared.
Therefore let me be wise. Too much
Of love's familiarising touch
Sours the whole story. Let me grow
Not into Lear but Prospero,
A kindly magic not imposed
But present when the scene has closed,
A backcloth to your growing acts,
A light that, flickering round the tracts
You trace, sets friendly signals on
The darkway each must walk alone.

Old Woman killed by Wild Bees

Sir, when death has dignity, one can concede
Its strict economy,
But this account is not well made; indeed
Whatever way to die
Invented could be more grotesque, malevolent
Than this obscenity out of black heaven sent?

A thousand little animals killing a greater,
This seems to be, is all.
No imaged godhead here – the massacred feature,
Dark heaving seething pall –
Surely some juggernaut we have deified,
Or justly doubt, Sir, that your loved one died.

Senile

Why should the inconsequent
Become their punishment,
The attractive caprices
Be fixed as vices,
A childish self-will
Appear so horrible?

In my beginning
Is my ending
Here is literal
And goes for all,
Beauty, charm, grace,
One savaged face,

Drained of all else,
Through one choked, clogged pulse.
Did you wish good
Or evil? The mood
Is clipped like a tag
On the four-limbed ragbag,

Dumped here to end
What nothing can mend
Or change, worn out
Clods, bundled about
Till a push more or less
Makes nothingness,

And death, like a frost,
Too late, lost,
Feigns dignity, silence
From the muddled violence
Of what love began
As a woman, as a man.

Harvester

The paint-red monster in a night-blue field,
Steaming a little as it goes to sleep,
While on hot metal the long-feared raindrops fall,
And the last labourer heaves his collar up,
Sloping closer to hedge – suddenly the scene
Is fixed and epic: harvest all is done,
Gathered, bound, dumped there by mechanical arms,
But still Tess labours late into bitter dark,
D'Urberville throws a deeper shadow down,
Angel is exiled by restraint and pride,
The rustics point and talk, but cannot save,
The stars rise sharp and tremble into pity,
A heartstrung sound travels the upland waste,
And the frail master outfaces the cold Presiders.

Sarah Siddons' Grave: Paddington

Old as she was, when she spoke, the teacups stopped;
Famous men with a mouthful of toast would choke
And swallow dumbly, watering at eyes, for fear
To nibble a noise in that deep cathedral tone:
Lady Macbeth in a lace mob-cap, she ruled them
By her own fireside, as in the candlelit theatre
With the great actors, she cowed and haunted the mind
Of all who heard or saw.
                                        And now she lies
Under plain stone in a playground, locked in the cage
Stamped with her name, like an eagle in an aviary
That never seems to appear though it must be there.
So, we think, must she be; the two carved words
Without profession, not even 'Actress', speak to us
Still in the cold wind, caught with tears in our eyes.

The Middle-Aged Man

Neighboured in plywood cubicles we stripped,
Put on identical clothes, the linen sheet
Slit for its head-hole like an Egyptian priest,
Over its stiff seams pulled the grey-tent gown,
Then sat like boxers or hurt football players
Bare-shinned on the hard bench, the middle-aged man
Whose name they took before mine, though not before
Some conversation keeping up the heart
Revealed us common friends, a cricket-club
We both had played for, small coincidences
Of a small town. Once only, at a mention
Half-joking, clumsy in our predicament,
He spoke of what had brought him into hospital:
'I've left it too late" he said.
                                        His name was called.
We parted, went through needful indignities,
Resumed our clothes, at different times dismissed,
Left without further goodbye. I heard his name
A fortnight later by the boundary line
Of a village green. 'They sent him home. Yes, dead.
Died in a few days. Wonder if he knew.'
I wonder too at what I did not know
Then in the linen sheet, the casual words
Too late now – 'I've left it too late', he had said –
The middle-aged man, the same age as my own.

Stillbirth

Between two worlds, of blood and air,
You lost your way. We soften this
In saying it. You died. There is
Nothing except the chemistries
Of chance accountable to wrong.

Love was your sole environ there.
The world of mother's blood you knew
Nine months, at one: you her, she you:
Think, in the world of air, how few
Can love so closely or so long.

Farm Boys Burning Stubble

Tow-headed, rag in hand,
Gnarled imps arson the land;
Human rooks, their cackled cries
Circle spits of sacrifice,
While their victims, mouse and lark,
Fear-mauled, flotsam the dark.

Evening gone, the field burnt,
These, torrid lesson learnt,
Mount iron, splinter the night
With steel vultures' wheeled flight;
Leathered still in killing mood
Leave the lanes bagged with blood.

Dead Bullock

Like a wild steer in death,
Raised horn, twisted neck,
The shocked carcass of beef
Slumps by the railway track.
Unsought, this blow forestalls
The blunt hammer of slaughter,
Cheating the back-street shambles
And blood-flushed abattoir.
Pasturing the wrong slope,
A flash flung him earthed
Down upon earth, black drape
Of sacrifice unwreathed,
Ungarlanded – with only
The rough clump of flowers,
He craned to feed on, thinly
Crowning his fly-crawled ears.

Botanic Gardens, Cambridge

This could be Eden: creatures in pairs,
Our own and early stamping-ground,
Mesopotamian growths, and look
Of a loving advent everywhere,
The raw sun rolling from mist-beds,
For the first day, we hand-in-hand,
Until a swan, our loneliness,
Scissored in half the blue-edged air.

Toosh

I spell his nickname as we spoke it, Toosh.
His name, we never used, was Tyldesley, born,
I guess now, in some Pennine-backed vicarage,
The populated graveyard for a playground,
The bells for nursery tunes. They put his school-bed
Under the window peering next to Chapel,
A pointed slit above a praying head
In a non-praying dormitory. Lights out:
The prefect had to push him off his knees.
He never spoke much; sometimes crossed himself
When smiled at; looked a scarecrow, long black hair
Like an old tramp or Christ, walked always alone
With dipping step. One day he disappeared
After a week of influenza. Roll-call
Buzzed with the news. That night they brought him back,
Picked up, running and muddy. Why, God knows,
They put him in the dormitory. On his bedside
He sat, shivering hard, a big sick bird,
His crow's head damp with clots. He stared, stared
Right through the puzzled prefects; not a sound.
They coaxed him to lie down; he did not budge.
Lights out. The rest of us slipped half-under, watched,
Trying to will it away. The Chapel bell
Hammered out ten with every beat a blow.
Toosh wafted up, dipped ghostly past my bed
Out in the corridor. Silence: a rush of feet,
Then yelling like a medieval hell.
Toosh had thought he was God, and tried to fly

To heaven, dragging the housemaster. The prefects pulled
them
Back through a landing window. All that night
The cries – was there no morphia in the place? –
But in the sleepless morning, a stripped bed,
And forty boys who did not look or speak.

Antony and Cleopatra

freely based on Chaucer

from The Legend of Good Women

Antony and Cleopatra

After the death of Ptolemy, the king
That over Egypt had the governing,
There reigned his widow Cleopatara,
Until it was ordained, as such things are,
That from the city of Rome a senator
Was sent to conquer kingdoms, and the power
Of Rome, as was the custom then, to raise
And have the world bow down to Roman ways.
All men may know, Antonius was his name.
As it fell out, he brought it down to shame,
For at the height of his prosperity,
A rebel to the town of Rome was he,
And above all, the Emperor Caesar's sister
He jilted her, and falsely he dismissed her,
And wished to make another woman wife.
So between him and Caesar there was strife.
Nevertheless, this same great senator
Was a most worthy noble warrior.
That he was doomed to die, it was most sad,
For love it was that made him halfway mad
And bound his greatness in a narrow snare
All for the love of Cleopatra.
The whole world else he reckoned valueless,
And thought his single duty nothing less
Than love and serve his Cleopatra's charms.
He only cared to risk his life in arms
In the defence of her and of her right.
The noble queen, she loved him too, her knight,

Both for his merit and his chivalry.
For certainly, unless the stories lie,
He, in appearance and in gentleness,
And in wise judgment and in hardiness
Was equal anyone, of any day:
And she was fair as is the rose in May.
And so, to cut a long tale short, soon she
Became his wife, just as she wished to be.
Their wedding and the feast I'd tell to you,
But I have many stories still to do.
When one takes on a project such as this,
Rather than be too long, and have to miss
Anything else more weighty and more large –
As men may overload a ship or barge –
So to the point of the story I will skip,
And the remaining pieces just let slip.
The Emperor Caesar, angry at this deed,
Raised against Antony a host to lead
All-out to bring about his overthrow:
Cruel as a lion was this Roman foe.
To ship they went, and so we see them sail.
Now Antony was not the man to fail
To face these Romans in a fighting way.
He made his plans, and, on a certain day,
He and his wife, with all their host, set out
Swiftly on shipboard, and, as it came about,
There, in mid-sea, they and the Romans met.
The trumpet sounds. They shout; and on they set,
Firing the first shots with the rising sun.
With grisly sound goes booming the big gun.

Fiercely they board each other, all at once;
From the maintop they hurtle down great stones.
Around the ropes each one the grapnel crooks
To slash them through with sharp-edged shearing-hooks.
Waving a pole-axe, presses every one:
Behind the mast the foemen dodge and run,
In and out, until overboard they leap
With stinging spears to pierce them in the deep.
With curving scythes they rend the sails apart,
While some bring drinks to give the men more heart.
Peas, thrown upon the hatches, make men slither,
And pots of quicklime blind them altogether.
And so the whole long day in fight they spend,
Till, at the last, since everything must end,
Antonius is defeated, put to flight,
And all his men disperse, as well they might.
The Queen fled too, with all her purple sail,
Under these strokes that fell as thick as hail
No wonder that she could not last it out.
And when Antonius saw this come about,
'Alas,' cried he, 'That ever I was born –
Now must my reputation look forlorn!'
In such despair his wits begin to go,
And with his sword he pierces his heart through,
And where he was defeated, dropped down dead.
His wife, from Caesar in distress and dread,
Back into Egypt fled across the ocean.
But listen, you who speak of true devotion,
Especially men, who falsely swear you'll die
Whenever your sweetheart treats you hurtfully,

Here you can see how women keep their faith.
For woeful Cleopatra used her breath
In lamentation such as no tongue tells;
And, the next day, waiting for nothing else,
She bade her subtle workmen make a shrine
Of rubies and of precious stones, as fine
As in all Egypt could be paid the price;
Then filled the shrine with every kind of spice
To embalm Antony's corpse: this she had fetched,
And in the shrine was his dead body stretched.
Next to the shrine she had a pit dug deep;
Then snakes and serpents of all kinds that creep
She put within that pit; and then she said:
'Now, O my love, whom my sad heart obeyed
So thoroughly, that from those blissful hours
When I first swore that I was wholly yours,
You, my Antonius, my knight, O you
That, sleep or waking, all the long day through,
Never my heart forgot, for any chance,
For good or ill, for singing or for dance,
For with myself this bargain made I still,
That everything you felt, for good or ill,
As far as ever it lay within my power,
As much as any wife may do, and more,
That too would I experience, life or death.
Now this same bargain, while I still have breath,
I shall fulfil, and well it may be seen
That, to her love, was never a truer queen!'
With these words, unprotected, deliberately,
Down in the pit, among the serpents, she

Leapt: thus she chose to have her burial.
Swiftly the adders and the serpents all
Stung her to death; but this she bravely faced,
For love of Antony her death embraced. –

Now this is history-truth: it is no fable.
Before you find a man so true and stable,
Freely willing to die for true love's sake,
I see that someone's head is going to ache!

The Gunboat

The Gunboat

This is a story of love and death, and a lake
So deep, the fishermen dropping their weighted lines
Never touch stone or rocky sand: for the earth
Breaks hollow there, some buried rift in the crust
Enough to cavern a monster or swallow a ship,
And this is the story.

A hundred years ago,
Italy, singing country of lemon and vine,
Stank like a dungeon. Uniforms strutted and clicked,
Foreigners gave the orders, prison or death,
Austrian voices, Austrian soldiers, Austria
Flying its clawing eagle flag in the blue
Darkened the sunlight. Only one half of the lake
Among the mountains still was free; there a man
Could steal a boat, and skilfully paddle, and land
Where a shaded light gave signal, so to escape
The tyrant bloodhounds leashed by the grim police
To the free side of the lake with peace and laughter,
Until the gunboat came.

That was a stroke
To startle and crush. 'We'll show these lying Italians,'
So the Austrian engineers, sweating and blond,
Dragged the bright sections by mule-back over the
mountains,
Fitting the parts like a jigsaw, and there it lay,
Squat scorpion, grey paint sizzling in the heat,

Bristling with shells and ugly turrets, a warship
Steaming its menacing plume on the peaceful lake.
That was an end of resistance: few tried it. The boat
Slipping across in the darkness, pretending to fish,
Seeking a friendly lantern, was suddenly framed
In the white shock of a searchlight: all at once spoke
The guns in an orange bellow. Some broken planks
And a fisherman's bonnet, pitiable disguise,
Were all that traced the spot, as the swordfish monster
Circled once, then steamed away, satisfied.

Now in Verona, Austrian-held, the Count,
Young, handsome, the secret hope of many in Italy,
Took a bride, she too Italian, and known
Like him to hate the tyrants. Then, what horror
To loyal friends and Italians, the Count announces
His honeymoon plans, to charter the Austrian gunboat
And cruise on the lake, to use their murder-ship
As a pleasure steamer. Austrian permission
Was easily granted for this, a fine demonstration
Better even than guns, to show the Italians
Their noble leader forgot all plot of revolt
In love, for love would tread his enemies' deck
And fly the flag of his love at their conquering masthead.
But the Italians – what fury and scorn when they saw
Not only the Count and his bride aboard, but found
Themselves the guests, feast under awnings, the guns
Pushed back, festooned with pennants and flowers, the
    ship
Blazing with lights beneath a velvet sky,

And the Austrian crew, drinking the wedding toast,
While the Count and his bride, like a slender lily, stood
    there
Receiving and bowing among this foreign court
Of men who had sent Italian blood to death.
And yet this was not the worst. For every nightfall
The gunboat anchored abreast a different town
On the rocky shore of the lake. The Count's invitation
Summoned aboard all families; loathing, they came
To another feast, each longer than the first,
More lavish with wine and healths to the happy couple,
Drunk deep by guffawing Austrian sailors, drunk
Sour between gritted teeth by the bitter Italians,
Who stayed no more than for sober politeness, then left
Muttering as their servants rowed them ashore.
Still smiling, the two young lovers stood at the rail
Waving good-bye, blind, infatuate, while
The drunken Austrians finished the food and the wine.

So the wedding cruise went on, one week, two,
Three, till the angry guests at each fresh night
Murmured openly now that the young Count's fortune
Would soon be spent, and many wished him that evil,
Till the garlanded gunboat came to the deepest part
Of all the long lake. Here hundreds of guests were bidden
From miles around. The invitations were pressing.
The guns on the boat, though shrouded, still were guns.
No one dared to refuse. But rage in their hearts
Grew high at the gross, most huge of festivities;
When early the foreign crew were drunk, insulting,

Staggering, and the Count, like a courteous host,
Took the chief Austrians below, put them to bed
With lengthy care, returned to the upper deck
With bland apologies, while the Italians glared
At him and his bride, and barely pressed the glasses
To moisten their lips.

And so it was that soon
Only Italians were left on the deck. And these,
The last of their vile invaders now drunk below,
Needed no cause to stay; nor did the Count
Nor the bride detain such a scowling company,
Feeling contempt in each brief touch of handshake,
Seeing the flash in the eye, as more than one guest
Spat as he swung down the gunboat side, and dropped
Into the boats that swiftly rowed them ashore.
And all, looking back with curses, saw, as always,
The Count and the young slim girl, his arm round her
waist,
Standing there at the stern-rail, silent, motionless,
Alone now.

Grumbling, the guests moved, up mountain paths
And dark herb-scented walks, each one toward home,
Leaving the black lake. Then, with a blinding flash
Never yet known on that water, the lake lit up,
And a bellowing roar like a beast in agony, hit
And hammered the cliff with echoes. Everyone turned
To the ship – the ship! There, over the deepest grave
Of the whole deep lake, in a burial sheet of flame

Tilted the ship on its death-dive, the flower-fed guns
Exploding in horrible heat, destroying itself
With its own infernal engines. For the Count, who took
Such time below with the drunk incapable crew,
Had stoked red-hot the boilers, let out the water,
And primed the ship to a pulse of death. And still
Ringed with that terrible flame, the two at the rail
Stood clasped, the Count and his bride. They had done,
from the first,
What they meant to do. They had put the devilish boat
In the deepest hole of the lake. They had done it alone,
Without help of friends, without love of friends, alone
With only their love to join them. And, joined in love,
The watchers upon the hillside saw how that honeymoon
Ended: the small groups everywhere fell to their knees
In congregation beneath the church of the stars:
'Gesu, Maria, what kind of a love was here!'

That was a story of love and death and a lake:
Of a lake so deep, and a love so deep, the mind
Cannot imagine, nor any eye trace its depth,
So deep it lies beyond dredging: not even a nail
From a rusty boat nor a ring from a wedding finger.

The Secret Mistress

The Secret Mistress

Macnamara, a Regency rake, lived at the foot of the Black Mountains. In his old age, he kept a mistress in a remote house called Hermitage. He visited her by coach over the hill-pass.

I. THE JOURNEY OUT

Cyclops-eyed, the coach wheels round
Into the courtyard's slushing sound,
Soft in mud and hard on grit,
The horses, fighting the swerving bit,
Fetch the half-circle, halt and shiver,
Rain on their watershed flanks a river,
Waiting for one who waits for death,
The prisoner in the noose of breath.

Now a new flame spatters out
Landing and window, weaves about
Oily and angry, tossed and blown,
A figure bulking slowly down,
Black doublewalker on the stair,
Misshapen shadows gambolling there,
Waiting for one who waits for death,
The prisoner in the noose of breath.

Shawled into darkness, stiff and old,
Shrugged under greatcoats, fold on fold,

Buried except for a frightened eye,
Age's gross anonymity,
Nerves and limbs their grinding dance:
The horses stamp in sodden trance,
Waiting for one who waits for death,
The prisoner in the noose of breath.

Sudden the threshold curbs his way,
A lowered bull he paws at bay,
Daunted by weather, stops; and then
Dives horn-first into the coach's pen.
Stir of hoof and groaning wheel:
He settles in the silk-lined cell,
Waiting for one who waits for death,
The prisoner in the noose of breath.

Climbing the valley, meet the storm,
Bent round the hillside's crooked arm;
The mountain track roars like a sluice;
Creatures of upper air are loose,
Howling for him the coach protects,
Whose need this journeying night selects,
Waiting for one who waits for death,
The prisoner in the noose of breath.

His thoughts, divided as his mind,
Straddle the miles, before, behind,
Ahead to love, still half-unsure,
Backward behind his own slammed door,
The angry wife, ungiving, old,

Walled in with silence, righteous-cold,
Waiting for one who waits for death,
The prisoner in the noose of breath.

One draws, one drives him on his way,
Yet neither claims the final say;
The secret mistress of his brain
Drags him out through black-rodded rain,
The thought that beckons white with bone,
Decay's pendulum skeleton,
Waiting for one who waits for death,
The prisoner in the noose of breath.

Not body's desire but body's dread
Plucks him from unquiet bed to bed,
The travel fever known to those
Who fly from every heart-beat's close:
Stand still, and each imagined drop
Creeps soft round to the pulses' stop,
Waiting for one who waits for death,
The prisoner in the noose of breath.

Anywhere but in the cage of stone,
Whose morticed ribs recall his own,
He trundles out, all judgment gone,
A speck that lumbers inchmeal on,
Over the wind-flat ridgeback grass,
Half-mad to all who watch him pass,
Waiting for one who waits for death,
The prisoner in the noose of breath.

Habit, like a hurt animal,
Seeks dark shelter in which to crawl;
Less reason than the working mole,
Blind-guided to a safer goal,
He feels the channel he must delve
Where the packed earth-banks spill and shelve,
Waiting for one who waits for death,
The prisoner in the noose of breath.

So in the tunnels of the night
Only the beasts reflect his light,
The goat that skips his lust aside,
The wildcat with her mountain pride,
Weasel and stoat, eyeballs of prey,
Green pointers to his groping way,
Waiting for one who waits for death,
The prisoner in the noose of breath.

Can love release his trembling route
From the doomed skirmish of the brute?
What single person can undo
The myriad coil we travel through?
No sign: unless one pinpoint fleck,
One rescue-beam in time's bare wreck,
Waiting for one who waits for death,
The prisoner in the noose of breath.

II. HERMITAGE

She walks, an upright wand.
She straightens with her hand

Reflecting silver and the froth of lace.
Outside the air skims by:
Inside her kingdoms lie,
And for his coming all must be in place.

Her senses make him lord,
Her loyalties afford
No room for reason or the world's sick tongue
Droning: 'Why wall alive
With one who will not wive
Beauty that cannot last for ever young?'

As actors in a play
Make artificial day
More bright and sharp than the bare sunlight can,
So she, lamp-centred here,
Creates the seasoned year
A paradise for readmitted man.

Nor is her play unreal.
Moved by a mute ideal
Beyond the mere spectator's grasp or glance,
Love nurtures its own scheme,
And who shall say the dream
Less true that minds' articulate advance?

For what seems madness in
The sober view, or sin
To rigid eyes, is nothing but a fact
In heartways handed down

With language of its own,
Before false babel severed word from act.

So in the pealing night
She shows her steadfast light
To guide a lover's criss-cross staggering path,
Where packs of howling dark
Leap wolfish to their mark.
A sanctuary from world and weather's wrath –

Tears off the shapeless years,
Cradles the sobbing fears,
Takes all remorse, all pity to her breast:
The face within the flesh
Shines through its sensual mesh,
The silver-minted coin that joy impressed.

Locking his head, she smooths
The features back to youth's,
Saying: 'My wildboy, my far-journeying man,
How can you call that old
Which can defy the cold,
The night, and even death's malicious plan?

I will protect you, I,
Though all around us die,
The battering moth and the plume-frozen bird.
Take my eternal food
And use it for your good,
Often and full as wish may name the word.'

So murmuring at his side,
She rouses manhood pride,
The strength and pinion of a towering lover,
With tattered wings to tear,
Mingle and tangle there,
He the broad buzzard, she the slim windhover.

Then calm as an old song
That sings of deep-laid wrong
Led by the hand of love to time's release,
She knits with slender things
His thick-grained ponderings,
Passing them through the small needle-eye of peace.

His now the starlit flower,
Perfection of an hour,
The break in cloud, the navigating moon,
Whose white touch on his sleeve
Tells him: 'None can bereave
Earth's quality, let death come late or soon.'

While she, her role fulfilled,
As pulse instinctive willed
Becomes the background to his drowsy spirit,
Her final fluttering wave
A passport through the grave,
An heirloom that no ghost can disinherit.

So, settled once again,
Though the blurred windowpane

Bear the returning traces of the storm,
His backward-looking trance
Still clings to her last glance,
As over every limb her love lies warm.

Jogged to an infant sleep,
With recollections deep
As all past life, he puts the future by,
While where the trackways bend
She watches to the end,
Till the last corner snuffs the flame-shot eye.

Then coldly to her rest,
She hugs, child to her breast,
Something achieved, some respite-comfort given,
A soul reached through the maze
Unthreaded but by her ways,
Youth's gift to Age, its later news of heaven.

III. THE JOURNEY BACK

The horses' slip, the waking stumble,
Upon the pass the wheels rumble –
Thunder, Macnamara, thunder!
Or is it warning, volleying wide,
Above, at hand, on every side,
Or under, Macnamara, or under?

Steeds of the night, why do you drive so quickly,
Mane-flying horses sweeping across the moon?

What do you drag that swallows the last poor glimmer,
Whose are those hands, the pale-set charioteer?
Is it the mist that straddles these mountain giants,
Drawn from the coach, the coachman, the flickering lamp,
Or have they life, or yet a more ghastly being,
The nightmare loose from its roots, the anatomied fear,
The features he dare not see, nor the voice dare hear?

The clouds wheel up, a waterspout,
The mountains shudder to its shout –
Strange tongues, Macnamara, strange tongues.
The world is breathing with dead breath,
And every breath it fills with death
Your lungs, Macnamara, your lungs.

Choking, shaking, painfully waking to living,
As once, a foot-long foetus, he left the womb
To set out all unwarned on the weird adventure,
Wailing from bloodshot darkness to milky cloud,
Never by choice, never by act of reason
Permitted to know the where and why of command,
Placed in the naked gate to sharpest encounter,
Weaponless but for the will to petition aloud,
Fitted to perish and matched to measure a shroud.

Dazed by the beat, the deadly drum,
How can the soaked-through senses come
To terms, Macnamara, to terms?
When the furred caterpillars of the rain,
Tadpoling down the window-pane,
Are worms, Macnamara, are worms?

Where now is Love, the pinpoint over the valley,
The dove thrown out in the storm, the rainbowed moon?
Love, alas, is behind the tabletop mountain,
Sunk in the trough where the snouted appetites mock.
Love, that is gentle, has no resources for brutedom,
Love, that is kind, has always the cruellest task,
To believe, to trust, and always to be defeated,
Ready for all but mortality's murderous shock –
Love with its timeless longings trapped by the clock.

Love that with bodies goes to bed
By those same bodies will be dead
And gone, Macnamara, and gone;
Though limbs a thousand ways embrace,
The last white grapple they must face,
Alone, Macnamara, alone.

Slowly and soft, with crepuscular deadly insistence,
Snowflakes' funnelling drift comes dizzying down,
Blinding the windows with pad of the packing shovel,
Burying, closing, entombing the frozen breast
Shrunk to a nutshell fear; the heartbeats shudder
In the shut box, at gasp for the bursting clot
That clogs the machine with blood of its own suffusing,
The toy that has jerked through its motions jammed at
last,
The key, if there was one, lost, its amusement past.

Yet this is not the end of all,
Only foretelling of the fall,

A sign, Macnamara, a sign
That men may hope as well as fear.
Fear is true hell: yet hope is near
Divine, Macnamara, divine.

For now the descending jolt shatters the veiling,
The eyes he imagined earthed are dazzled to see
The dawn-sun strike its blow from the line of the hilltop,
The valley shivered with lightshine, whitened but gay,
Himself alive, and familiar portions of daybreak,
Crowing and clinking of iron and shuffle of feet,
Show that men once again are stubborn and willing.
Though sleep warn death, they endeavour for one more day
To shoulder the ponderous world on its unknown way.

A mistress's love that lasts the night
Counterparts the courageous sight
Of men, Macnamara, of men,
Who in a life they did not ask
Walk cheerful out to their doomed task
Again, Macnamara, again.

Early labourers, seeing the steam-close windows,
Make their grimaces, coarse as the dung-dropped yard.
The sun gilds all. It edges his dream returning
Of her, though remote, her wraith of comfort still near.
Soon its upstanding ray will fall on her hermitage
As on his solitary castle. So the soul
And body may be by brilliant moments united,
And each half-life in its different hemisphere
Find wholeness in knowing another it holds more dear.

The movement ends, the hooves stopped,
The tired horses, their heads dropped,
Are home, Macnamara, are home.
Man has been out, and now is back,
Fortressed until the next attack
Shall come, Macnamara, shall come.